DREAM JOBS If You Like VIDEOS

by Amie Jane Leavitt

CAPSTONE PRESS
a capstone imprint

Capstone Captivate is published by Capstone Press, an imprint of Capstone.
1710 Roe Crest Drive
North Mankato, Minnesota 56003
www.capstonepub.com

Library of Congress Cataloging-in-Publication Data is available on the Library of Congress website.
ISBN: 978-1-4966-8400-4 (library binding)
ISBN: 978-1-4966-8451-6 (eBook PDF)

Summary: Wouldn't it be cool to have a job working with or around the things you love? Do you wish you could get paid to make movies? Maybe a job as a camera operator or set designer is the right direction! Readers will discover the possibilities of careers working with videos.

Image Credits
Alamy: Edmund Sumner-VIEW, 28; Capstone Studio: Karon Dubke, Cover; Getty Images: Caspar Benson, 13; iStockphoto: DGLimages, 7, Felix Seichter, 12, Goodboy Picture Company, 17, ollo, 9; Shutterstock: ArtHead, (circuit pattern) Cover, FrameStockFootages, back cover, 11, 21, 26, frantsev, 19, Martin Vorel, 15, MIKHAIL GRACHIKOV, (dots) Cover, PHILIPIMAGE, 22, sirtravelalot, 25, SVRSLYIMAGE, 5

Editorial Credits
Editor: Heather Williams; Designer: Sara Radka; Media Researcher: Morgan Walters; Production Specialist: Spencer Rosio

All internet sites appearing in back matter were available and accurate when this book was sent to press.

Printed in the United States
PA117

Table of Contents

Words in **bold** are in the glossary.

There are millions of jobs in the world, but only a few are dream jobs. A dream job might not make you rich or famous, but you'll be excited to go to work every day. If you love watching movies or making your own films or music videos, one of these might be your dream job!

Video creators sometimes use a selfie stick to help them make videos of themselves.

Video Creator

The internet is filled with all kinds of videos. Some show people traveling the world. Others show people cooking or building. Video creators make these videos.

On the Job

Video creators tell a story or show a special event. They teach people how to do something. The camera is the most important tool a video creator has. Some video creators put cameras on **drones** to film **aerial** shots. Video creators often add special effects to their videos. They can record in slow motion. They use computers to add music. Most video creators spend many hours **editing** their **footage**.

FUN FACT

A vlogger is a person who regularly posts videos to vlogs. These are online video channels. Some of the highest paid vloggers make about $18 million per year.

Pay Range

Pay in this job can range from nothing to around $100,000 per year. Online video platforms often pay video creators per viewer click.

Education and Skills

Some video creators go to college. They study film and video production. Others learn on the job. They might work with **mentors**. They must know how to use their cameras. They must understand lighting and sound. They must also know how to use computer programs for editing. Video creators should know about internet marketing too. This will help them attract more people to their work.

Producer

Producers rarely star in a film or TV show. They do not act, sing, or dance. Their job is behind the scenes. They are in charge of the business side of making films.

On the Job

Producers have many jobs. First, they find ideas for films. Then, they hire screenwriters to write the **scripts**. These are the stories that will be told in the movies or TV shows. Producers figure out how much it will cost to make a film. Then, they find **investors**. These people provide money to make films. Producers must get the OK to film in certain places. They hire the director, cast, and crew. Then, they set up a production schedule. This tells when all of the scenes will be filmed. Producers work with the director to make sure this schedule is kept. They also keep a close eye on the budget. Producers are often in charge of marketing too. They need to get people excited about the film.

FUN FACT

Steven Spielberg is one of the most successful filmmakers in history. He is both a producer and a director. He applied to film school twice but was not accepted. But he did not give up. He worked for free as an intern at Universal Studios. He learned the ins and outs of the film industry from the ground up.

Pay Range

Depends upon the film and budget. The average is between $40,000 and $131,000 per year.

Education and Skills

Many producers go to college. They study film and acting. They also take classes in business and communications. Producers must be good with money. They must pay attention to details. Producers know how to get tasks done on time. They are good managers. They know how to put together and lead a team. They are also creative people who know a good idea when they see one!

Producers watch over all the parts of a production, including the filming, set, and schedule.

Director

Directors are the creative people who lead the making of a film or TV show. They are in charge of everything seen on the screen. They work with the actors and crews. They also work with producers.

On the Job

Directors work on many types of projects. They work on movies and TV shows. They also work on **documentaries**. Directors have many jobs. First, they read a script. They decide how it will look on the screen. They help the producer choose the actors who will play the parts. They also give suggestions on where the film should be shot. Directors work with other members of the crew. They pick the costumes worn by the actors. They give tips to help actors give their best performances. Directors figure out how a scene will be set up. They tell where the furniture and props should go. Directors also explain how the final film should look.

Pay Range

Depends upon the film and budget. Some experienced directors make millions of dollars per year. The average is around $111,000.

Sometimes, a director uses a real place to create a scene in a movie.

Education and Skills

Most directors go to film school. They study filmmaking and performing arts. They also learn about the technical part of filmmaking. They learn about lighting, camera equipment, and the editing process. They need to be good communicators so they can share their ideas with others. They must also have a good imagination. This lets them picture how the words in a script can turn into a film.

FUN FACT

Alfred Hitchcock was a famous director of suspense movies. He often made **cameo** appearances in his movies. Audiences knew he would show up somewhere in the movie. Sometimes his cameo was simply a photo in a newspaper or book.

Video Editor

At the end of filming, directors usually say, "That's a wrap!" This phrase means that filming is over. But it doesn't mean that the film is ready for people to see it. All the footage must go to a video editor. This person turns hours of film into a finished product.

On the Job

Video editors usually work in front of a computer. They look at all the footage that was shot. This is up to hundreds of hours for a movie. TV shows have much less footage. Editors turn this material into a complete video story using computer software. They look at the script to see the flow of the story. Then they piece together the footage. As they do this, they check for any problems that need to be corrected. They make sure the sounds match what is happening on the screen. They add the music and the graphics. They make sure the special effects match the script.

Pay Range

Between $30,000 and $170,000 per year, depending upon experience and skills.

Education and Skills

Many video editors go to college between two and four years. They study film or broadcasting. They know how to use video-editing software. They will often use many different types of software in their jobs. Video editors should have a good eye for detail. They must be able to spot issues that need to be changed. Video editors need to be able to follow directions. They will receive many instructions on the project from the film's director.

FUN FACT

On big feature movies, video editors are not allowed to tell anyone about the projects they are working on. Each project has a special name, called a working title. The working title for Marvel's 2012 movie *The Avengers* was "Group Hug."

A video editor spends many hours in front of a computer putting together a full-length movie or TV show.

Actors must be willing to travel to many locations to appear in movies and TV shows.

Actor

Actors entertain audiences by pretending to be someone else. They star in movies and TV shows. They also appear in TV commercials.

On the Job

Actors are hired to take on the role of a character. The character may be make-believe or based on a real person. Actors receive a copy of the script. The script tells the actors what they are to say and do in the production. Actors must memorize all of their lines. They must also learn all about their character. Actors are fitted for costumes. They get their hair and makeup done before they go on set. The set is the place where the scenes are acted out in front of the camera. A scene is usually acted out many times before it is just right.

Pay Range

Top actors can make millions of dollars per year. Average salary = $51.00 per hour.

Education and Skills

Actors often take acting or drama classes. Some have college degrees in performing arts and filmmaking. Others attend workshops taught by acting coaches. Sometimes, actors are asked to sing and dance. It is helpful if actors take classes in these areas as well. Actors must have good memories. This will help them learn their lines. They must also have good imaginations, since they have to take on many roles.

FUN FACT

During medieval and Renaissance times, women weren't allowed to be actors. Male actors played the parts of both men and women. The first female actors took the stage in England in 1660.

An actor often shares the stage with others and must be able to work as part of a team.

Lighting Technician

Have you ever taken a picture that was too dark or too bright? Then you know how important good lighting is. People called lighting technicians work behind the scenes on the sets of films and TV shows. They make sure the lighting is just right for the cameras.

On the Job

Lighting technicians work with film directors. The directors tell them what kind of lighting they want. The lighting techs set up the lights. They use many different types of light sources. They use regular, everyday lighting such as lamps and candles. These are generally part of the set where the actors perform. Lighting techs also use lighting that is placed high above the set. Overhead lighting is used for certain situations. Key lighting is one type of overhead lighting. It places lights on the main subject. Fill lighting is another. It removes dark and shadowy areas from a person's face. Backlighting is another. It helps create more of a 3-D scene. The lighting techs move lights by hand or with the help of a computer.

FUN FACT

The very first movies used mostly natural lighting. This is one of the reasons the film industry was based in the sunny state of California.

When a scene is filmed at night, a lighting technician must provide enough light for the camera to show the actors' faces.

Pay Range

Between $30,000 and $46,000 per year.

Education and Skills

Some lighting techs study electrical engineering in college. But most learn on the job. They study with experienced lighting techs to learn the trade. They must know about the many different types of lighting equipment used in filmmaking. They must be able to climb ladders and adjust lighting as needed. They must also be able to work with special equipment to raise and lower lights.

Screenwriter

Every film or TV program tells a story. The person who writes that story is the screenwriter. Screenwriters write scripts for the actors to follow. These scripts tell the lines the actors say. They describe the movements of the actors too. Scripts also tell the way the scene or set needs to be set up.

On the Job

Many screenwriters work from their offices in movie studios. Others work from home. Sometimes, they come up with their own ideas. They think about things that have happened in their lives. Or they think of things they have heard about in the news. Then, they turn their ideas into scripts. Screenwriters might also be asked to write a script based on a producer's idea. Screenwriters are not done when they write "THE END" on their manuscript. They are often asked to be on the set during production. Changes are often made during filming. Screenwriters help with those changes.

FUN FACT

The average movie script is between 110 and 120 pages long. Each page is equal to about a minute of the final film.

Pay Range

Depends upon the project and the writer's experience. The average is between $60,000 and $100,000 per year. However, it can also be much lower. Beginning screenwriters sometimes work for free.

Education and Skills

Not all screenwriters go to college. They should be good writers. They should also be creative people with good imaginations. Screenwriters should be good listeners and should pay attention to details. Being good observers helps them create interesting stories. They need to work hard and meet deadlines. They should have good communication skills. They will often work with other people and be team players.

Screenwriters spend many hours coming up with interesting, entertaining scripts for movies and TV shows.

Set Designer

Everything you see in a movie or show is there for a reason. The flowers in a garden were carefully chosen. So were the items piled high in a garage. They all tell a part of the film's story. Set designers are the people who create these scenes.

On the Job

Set designers first read a copy of the script. They then meet with the producers and the directors. They discuss the budget and story. Then they choose all the furniture and props for each scene. Sometimes, they work on location. They bring the props and furniture to decorate a house or building. At other times, they have to build a place from scratch. They sketch out what they want. Then, they give the plans to a construction team that builds the set. The set is a very important part of a show or movie. It helps the actors feel like they are part of the story. It also helps the audience enter the world of the story.

FUN FACT

Titanic had one of the most expensive movie sets of all time. Set designers built a copy of the actual ship. It was about 90 percent of the size of the real *Titanic*. It cost more than $30 million to build.

Pay Range

Between $21,000 and $61,000 per year, depending upon experience and where the job is located.

Education and Skills

Set designers often go to college. They study set design and theater. Some study fine arts and interior design. Set designers are creative people. They have a background in drawing. They also are good at working with a team. They are able to work within a budget and tight schedule. They often spend many long hours getting the sets finished before production begins.

Set designers supervise the construction of sets, and sometimes help with the building process.

Foley Artist

Watch a clip of your favorite movie. Pay attention to all the sounds you hear. They were created by a Foley artist. Foley artists have been making sounds for films since the 1920s. That's when sound was first added to movies. The job is named after Jack Foley. He was the first person to put sound effects in movies.

On the Job

Foley artists work in special kinds of sound studios. The studios have microphones and video screens. They are also stocked with a variety of everyday objects. Foley artists use these items to make sound effects for film clips. For example, a clip might include a fireplace. The Foley artists need to make the sound of fire crackling. They may crinkle an empty chip bag to make the crackling sound. They might twist a sheet of bubble wrap to make the sound of the logs popping. Foley artists use their own creativity to create common sounds in unusual ways.

FUN FACT

Foley artists use the sound of sizzling bacon to make the sound of rain.

Pay Range

Between $400 and $450 per day.

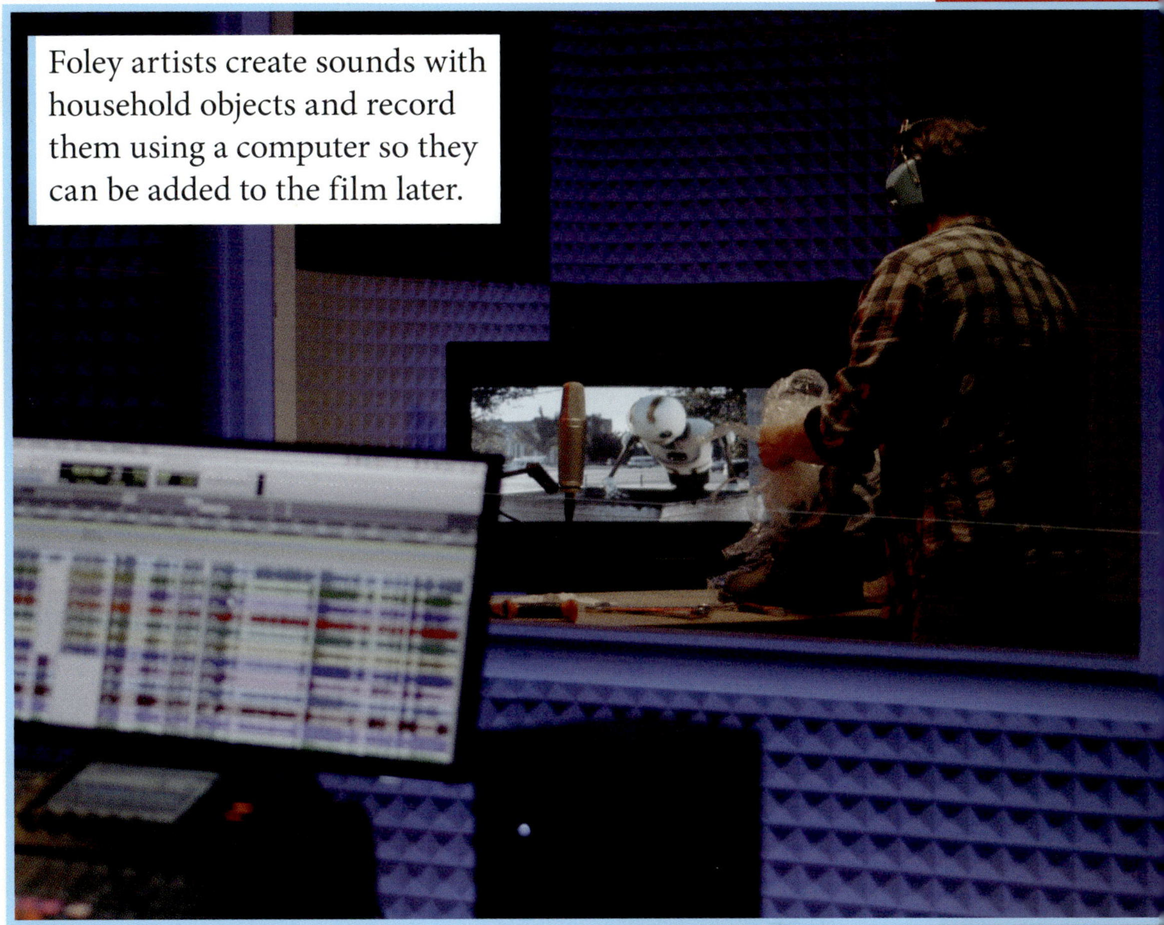

Foley artists create sounds with household objects and record them using a computer so they can be added to the film later.

Education and Skills

Foley artists don't have to go to college. However, many have a background in sound or recording. They might study sound engineering or film production. Many learn Foley art by being an **apprentice**. Foley artists see fine details and have sharp ears for sounds. They have good hand-eye **coordination**. They can see something on screen and quickly copy the movements. Foley artists must move fast to match sounds to what they see.

Camera operators must know how to use professional cameras with many buttons, microphones, and accessories.

Camera Operator

All types of videos need a person to run the camera. Some simple films have just one camera operator. Larger productions have a whole team. Camera operators work in news reporting, TV programs, and films.

On the Job

Camera operators work with production teams and directors. They find out what kinds of scenes need to be filmed. This helps them choose the right equipment. Closeup shots require a camera that can zoom in on the subject. Aerial shots require cameras that are mounted onto cranes or drones. Operators set up and move their cameras many times during filming. They constantly adjust for lighting. They must make sure the camera's view is in focus. Operators work many long hours. Movies are often shot from early in the morning until late at night. Operators often travel for work.

FUN FACT

Sometimes camera operators have to climb 50-foot (15 meters) towers to get high angles for shots.

Pay Range

Between $69,000 and $103,000 per year.

Education and Skills

Camera operators often go to college between two and four years. They study journalism, TV, or film. They know how to use camera equipment. They understand how lighting works. They also know how to get the best angles of a subject. They are often creative people who can think of many ways to solve problems. Camera operators must be team players.

Costume Designer

Actors usually don't wear their own clothing in a TV show or film. Neither do most singers in music videos. They wear costumes. Costume designers come up with the ideas for how to dress these performers.

On the Job

Costume designers tell details about a character through the clothes the actors wear. Designers read the script first. This helps them get an idea of the characters and setting. They meet with the directors and producers and find out their ideas for the costumes. Designers also find out the budget for the film. This lets them know how much they can spend on costumes. Once they have the basics, they get to work. They do research on the story's setting. This helps them find out what styles of clothing match that setting. They sketch out their designs and hire a team to make the costumes. The final step is making sure the costumes fit the actors.

Pay Range

Between $20,000 and $61,000 per year, depending upon on location and experience of the designer.

Education and Skills

Some costume designers go to college. They study costume and fashion design. Other costume designers learn by working. Designers must enjoy research. They must know how to communicate with others on a team. They must be creative people with good imaginations. They must also know how to work within a budget.

FUN FACT

The Chewbacca costume in *Star Wars* was extremely hot. The actor could hardly stand to stay inside it. So the costume designers added a special cooling system to the suit. This let the actor stay inside without roasting!

A costume designer chooses each part of an actor's costume carefully to make sure it matches the setting of the film or show.

CGI Artist

CGI stands for computer-generated imagery. This type of art is found in all sorts of places. A big battle scene in a movie is probably CGI. So is a visit to another planet or the sinking of a giant ship like the *Titanic*. CGI artists make **animations** and visual effects for videos, TV shows, movies, games, and more.

CGI artists often work as a team to create characters and scenes for animated movies.

On the Job

CGI artists work at a computer most of the day. Some work alone. Others work as part of a team. CGI artists design pictures and animations for videos. Some make cartoons or video games. Others work on the special effects and landscapes for movies. Some CGI artists work on documentaries. They help create scenes from history and science. They must do research and talk to experts. This helps make their work factual. CGI artists use computer programs to create their digital art. Often, they have to know computer programming languages. This lets them put their art into something a computer understands.

FUN FACT

Toy Story was the first feature film to be made entirely with CGI. It was released by Disney in 1995.

Pay Range

Average salary = $60,000 per year.

Education and Skills

Most CGI artists have a college degree. They usually study computer graphics or digital media. They are creative and love art. They are also good at doing research and finding facts. They work well on a team. Many CGI artists study fine arts in school. They also know how to use computers and video-editing software. They take classes on the latest software releases. This helps them do their jobs well.

Film archivists organize films in special storage vaults that protect films from light, extreme temperature, and moisture.

Film Archivist

Hundreds of thousands of movies have been made through the years. Many movies are made out of fragile material called film. Film is a strip of plastic that pictures are recorded on. Original copies of these movies need to be protected. Film archivists work at a library or museum. They keep the movies in the collection safe. This allows people to enjoy watching these pieces of history for many years to come.

On the Job

Movies recorded on film should not get too hot or too cold. They also can't be in a place that is too dry or too **humid**. Film archivists know the right way to store film. They keep the movies in special cold storage vaults. The vaults are kept at a set temperature and humidity. This keeps old film from falling apart. Archivists also make sure these movies are stored in a way that people can find them. They organize them much like books in a library. The movies have "call numbers" and are placed in a certain order on the shelves.

FUN FACT

Most of the silent movies made in the 1920s weren't stored properly. Because of that, many of them have already fallen apart. There are no other copies of them, so they are lost forever.

Pay Range

Average salary = $52,000 per year.

Education and Skills

Most film archivists go to college for at least six years. Some go longer. They study film. They also study library science. Film archivists love movies. They want to do something to save history. Archivists are good organizers. They have good communication skills and like working with a team.

Glossary

aerial (AYR-ee-uhl)—something that happens in the sky

animation (a-nuh-MAY-shun)—a cartoon made by quickly presenting drawings, one after another, so that the characters seem to be moving

apprentice (uh-PREN-tiss)—someone who learns a trade by working with a skilled person

cameo (KA-me-yoh)—a brief appearance by a celebrity

coordination (koh-OR-duh-NAY-shun)—using different parts of the body together, smoothly and in time

documentary (dahk-yuh-MEN-tuh-ree)—a movie or TV program about real situations and people

drone (DROHN)—an unmanned, remote-controlled aircraft

edit (EH-duht)—to remove all unnecessary parts from a film to create a finished product

footage (FUT-ij)—all of the scenes from a movie or TV show

humid (HYOO-mid)—damp or moist

investor (in-VESS-tur)—a person who provides money for a project in return for a share of the profits

mentor (MEN-tur)—a wise and faithful adviser or teacher

script (SKRIPT)—the story for a play, movie, or TV show

Read More

Bellmont, Laura. *Animation Lab for Kids: Fun Projects for Visual Storytelling and Making Art Move.* Beverly, MA: Quarry Books, 2016.

Blofield, Robert. *How to Make a Movie in 10 Easy Lessons: Learn How to Write, Direct, and Edit Your Own Film without a Hollywood Budget*. Mission Viejo, CA: Walter Foster Jr., 2015.

Kruse, Jeremy. *The Young Actors' Handbook*. Milwaukee, WI: Applause Theatre & Cinema Books, 2017.

Stoller, Bryan Michael. *Smartphone Movie Maker.* Somerville, MA: Candlewick Press, 2017.

Internet Sites

CGI for Kids
https://kids.kiddle.co/Computer-generated_imagery

Foley Art
https://www.pbs.org/video/whats-buzz-what-foley

Screenwriting for Kids
https://www.youtube.com/user/ScreenwritingKidsOK/videos

Videography
https://www.adorama.com/alc/how-to-become-a-videographer

Index